THE BARONS

Poetry

Severance Songs
(Tupelo Press, 2011)

Fourier Series
(Spineless Books, 2007)

Selah
(Barrow Street Press, 2003)

Fiction

Beautiful Soul: An American Elegy
(Spuyten Duyvil Publishing, 2014)

As Editor

The *Arcadia* Project: North American Postmodern Pastoral, with G. C. Waldrep.
(Ahsahta Press, 2012)

JOSHUA COREY
THE BARONS

OMNIDAWN PUBLISHING
RICHMOND, CALIFORNIA
2014

Cover Art:
CREDIT: © 2014 Artists Rights Society (ARS), New York / VG Bild-Kunst, Bonn

Beuys, Joseph (1921-1986) © ARS, New York. *Iphigenia/Titus Andronicus*. 1984.
Photographic negatives stamped with brown paint between glass plates in
iron frame, composition: 28 1/8 x 21 9/16" (71.4 x 54.8 cm).
Gift of Edition Schellmann, Munich and New York.
The Museum of Modern Art, New York, New York.
Digital Image © The Museum of Modern Art/
Licensed by SCALA / Art Resource, New York.

Book cover & interior design by Cassandra Smith

Offset printed in the United States
by Edwards Brothers Malloy, Ann Arbor, Michigan
On 55# Enviro Natural 100% Recycled 100% PCW
Acid Free Archival Quality FSC Certified Paper
with Rainbow FSC Certified Colored End Papers

Library of Congress Cataloging-in-Publication Data

Corey, Joshua.
  [Poems. Selections]
  The barons / Joshua Corey.
    pages ; cm
  ISBN 978-1-890650-98-8 (pbk. : alk. paper)
  I. Title.
  PS3603.O7343A6 2014
  811'.6--dc23
                              2014013752

Published by Omnidawn Publishing, Richmond, California
www.omnidawn.com   (510) 237-5472   (800) 792-4957
          10 9 8 7 6 5 4 3 2 1
          ISBN: 978-1-890650-98-8

Contents

I write poetry for the fucking stars.

—Robert Duncan

The Millions

THE MILLIONS

Epic fail and the man I sing
above the strip in the heat index
dead desiring dry tsunami
curtaining the buildings like fallout
drifting through corridors   tidal
sweeping sunglasses, crankshafts, I-beams
before it
(still itself the
wreckage amidst
the wreckage)
meanwhile staggering
on the zombie economy
tries to think itself out of its mind
like a small vicious strong-smelling
animal   say a mink
caught in the iron cage of its
natural habitat
we shamble until we stop or are
stopped
under the interchanges
abandoned cars strung out like beads
doors flapped open like tongues
shading eyes to the horizon
the catastrophe
squatting there with its million tongues
as if it were that simple to bear it to witness
the event
if I could get it in gear I
would   believe me
can't find the wound with my hands
but it's an arrow piercing me and
everyone
branching back in ragged feathers its
purer linearity thrust forward
between my daughter's eyes
back turned to webbed simultaneity

this morning thousands died
the evening's birth is universal
no I can't count that high
on my fingers and toes even
visual modeling makes a window
but I don't know the code
zeroes and ones fly by
adding up to the verb intelligence
"as for living, our hybrid vehicles
will do that for us"
the window's closing
on all that air and light
to render it spectacular and unusable
but for now nothing protects me
and I'm glad
to be the child of my place and time
the father too   I would make
a model   means of seeing   diorama
glued to a plank in reason
floating in whatever gutters are left
under a few stars
to document my failure
to secure and see the millions
find me midstream dragging a hand behind
grasping fishy Heraclitus
pulling me back and under
drowning my life and my life
together for a breath
counting cadence to survive
the work of open eyes

A PAINFUL CASE

Mist-wracked, mis-
abandoned the smaller
fields. Tall

as a train Cousin Steptoe
steps, snapping his suspenders
against his chest.

Show me your nipples,
Cousin Steptoe. Oblige
me, abrigato. He

obliges: they are corn-
curled pennies, buffalo
nickels when took of wing.

I have an animal in tow,
a close relation bred and born
in the global south:

he's a slipcase for a telephone.

The open dark
follows us down
North Clark. Easy loans,

tamale stands. Some
turn to track my stride,
his hand on his tail—

indecently, imperceptibly
a wrong. Take a tall
tack toward a tasteless

case of lumbago—antiquary
disease. My cousin mums

and palms:

he's avalanche recto typhoon verso.

Garnishing my salary
with a little celery
in the Don't-Despair-Just-Yet Office

waiting room, I sit
in Steptoe's lap—he's a grandfather
clock, I the bit of brass,

swingstarry, struck. His head's
a combination lock
inside this fortune

cookie, my mouth.
Which you parade,
Doctor Can't-See-You-Now.

Tapped out. The city beat. Subprime.

I like to died with Cousin
Steptoe. Outside, the yellow water.
Inside this number, soldier's joy, the paws.

COGNITIVE DEFICIT MARKET

She has forgotten what she forgot
this morning: her keys, toast in the toaster blackening
the insides of beloved skulls, little planetariums
projecting increasingly incomplete
and fanciful constellations: the Gravid
Ass, the Mesozoic Cartwheel, the Big
Goatee, the Littlest Fascist. Outside her window
a crowd gathers, seething in white confusion
like milk boiling dry in a saucepan—some
lift fingers to point this way and that
with herky-jerky certainty but
they're standing too close for all
those flying hands so that eyeglasses and hats
fall—apologies inaudible, someone hands
a fist, the brawl overwhelms the meager traffic
of pedicabs and delivery trucks stacked high
with rotting lettuce. Meanwhile above it all
she's setting out the tea things: ceramic cup and saucer,
little pewter spoon, pebbled iron pot, a slice
of Sara Lee. Waiting to remember
to turn the radio on, listen for the elevator, for
the lock to turn or a knock
on the door. In a little while she'll put everything
away in the same configuration
at the bottom of a clean white sink
with its faucet dripping.
We who watch this, half-turned away already
toward sunny gardens or the oncoming semi—
being not the one dead but not exactly alive either.
The skin is a glove that wrinkles as it tightens.
The cerebellum's the same. A game
of chess between walking sticks—I mean the insects
made up to resemble wood. I say we dissemble
from photographs to repeat
our stakes in weightless names.

IT GOES BY IN FLASHES, IT BOWS

> "It doesn't scare me to be the perfect human."
> —Jørgen Leth, *The Five Obstructions*

Farm work tunnels through Crèvecœur's imaginary—

The little outrageous—

The centerless misery my business is—

Apple-pied autumn, colder nights slow coming, eyes averted—

My child-to-be's rucksack—

Ordinary madness on the commuter train, the conductor can't sleep—

Many are skeptics toward the Gaia hypothesis—

What is a hypothesis? A left-handed spanner. Man's gold armature astride a Kawasaki hotbike—

I keep wanting to bite something big and hang on, like a tire—

Lips for babies—

The tenor leaks from my neighbor's earphones. Tourette's grunts and gasps, backs of hands ground into eyes—

Sax on leaves, the day—

The eyes a portal to infections—

Checked pants, "your bathroom's nasty!"—

Weaponized body I hurtle into age. As a widow takes in lodgers—

Flesh of the nineteenth century of my flesh. Accumulated—

The key is no motion, nor action, nor notion. Emphasize the apophatics—

"He was looking for you what were your scores it's good for you maybe you and I should go bowling sometime would you like to do that?" He says nothing. "Did you see Peter on the train?"—

The shore piles up to the left and right. The suburbs unchecked, rex—

Last pages before birth. "People might not know you the way I do, know what I'm saying? Like I know you. People may not realize that you're trying to get through—"

My loneliness fell away and shattered on the pavement. Hulks. We see what they are, the misshapen ones—

A line of tanks somewhere. A sentiment. Step down, the barricades—

"George Washington cannibalistically developed"—

"And if you don't like to shop it's okay. Peter?"—

He shuts down the flaps of his people-hunting hat and listens—

FAREWELL MY LOVELY

Monarch howl, caterwaul pinch,
who needs these animals? Gunnysack 'em.

Caution, Phil. You took a little spill.
I plucked you out of the hillside and set your hair on end.

Vocative O henceforth. A gesture moon.
Stain'd by a history of eyes, the man sallies

and rallies before the end: droppt elevator.
In the Mindful Building she props two gams on a desk.

Waving and drowning. The poem's alive
as your trigger finger. Pull the stranger.

On the corner of Catapult and Vine, a limo idles.
The driver leafing through *The Screwtape Letters*.

The passenger blots angry tears. "Take me
to the Hotel Figurine." Her status blares,

but I haven't a pot to piss in. Wait a
second, I found it. It was tucked

between the pages of my copy of *Medieval
Scenes*. That's better. Now to revise my fancy.

These homunculi, animalcules, writhing
soon as named. Even you in mind.

It's all a question of scale: the horn
duct-taped to a policeman's head.

Displaced persons assemble round a ringtone.
Parapoetics hands the Book of Kings to a bald barber.

Attend the tale, maestro. It's okay with me
if bachelor Barbies ring round the bonfire.

In the end, the detective is fully implicated
(*I believe they should be served with the head*)

and strikes a self-destructive blow for justice.
(*It is a ... creational passion that presides.*)

The body hurled from a cornering car
and tumbling in the weeds down the hillside.

Life as we knew it, my poor Philip.
You no longer figure in my schemes.

Competing, naked, ides of March.
The speeches and funeral games.

A wisp from a cigarette holder—so.
She stubbed out my toe and turned away.

COMPLETE ADVENTURES

I. In porcelain peril

This person sat smally kicking his legs against the stall while above him loomed the Looming Carl. This person could not meet the Carl's eye but went on shrilly kicking. The Carl was one of those people who assume that all other people feel just as they do; he had a toothache; he roared Open your mouth and opened his own; his tongue lolled horribly. This person bit his lip and kicked faintly the stall, which I might as well tell you was really the Carl's left shin. For why should we hold secrets from each other—from you, from this person, from I who write this beside a pot of yogurt at daybreak? I'll teach you, the Carl howled, beatings his mitts on the stall walls: and he did, and he did, and he did.

II. *In which we are transported*

An adverb to modify is, this person thought happily from his high chair.
He spooned some yogurt. The floor of Grand Central Station was far below
him and the black grains of the commuters' hats churned there like rice
on a tapped tin plate. Where's my Looming Carl, this person thought, and
then remembered: but it's my turn to loom. So this person did his level
little best, sitting up straight and shaking white glops of yogurt down on
the floor so far below, where they splatted contentedly on tiles and hatted
heads. A few squinted up but all they could see was the winter sun breaking
whitely through glass exactly at the nimbus of this person's haircut. I'm
an emergency, this person said excitedly, waving his spoon in the air. Then
soberly: An emergency all alone. Someone skidded on something white far
below and fell down in a pewter clatter. But this person didn't see, or else he
only heard. Heavenly hurt it gives us.

III. In memory of his feelings

Owaagh, the blurbs, this person said adversely to Senor Elbow, who nodded
briskly in time his sleek smallish head. I ate too many, Senor, this person
gasped, I'm pregnant luminously, necessarily, prominently, uncapturably. Just
the thing, murmured Elbow smoothly, I have for you. In the manner of a
master maitre'd, which he was. He turned aside to his dainty dental tray. He
flicked a set of lenses over this person's incisors. Better? Or worse? Owaagh,
urgh, this person replied. Again the Senor flicked his lenses, clicking like heels
in the manner of a matador. Better? I can't feel my faculty, this person cried.
And then: Worse! Senor flinched, flicked some more. Stop right there, this
person gasped. He threw back his head and sipped the air, then ripped off
the uncomfortably small leather mask, sniffling and snuffling great guffles. By
George, this person cried, and again, by George. I think you've got it, smiled
the Senor.

IV. *In an annex of the road*

If we get to elect our emperor then the real emperor must be someone else, this person thought. He sat upon a phone book full of the most recent polls. Hannibal's elephants climbed the Alps in a frieze outside the kitchen, where this person's egg salad sandwich dried out underneath a heat lamp. To dry out is to get sober, this person thought, sipping gin fizz through a straw. It was time to be nighthawks again and soon this person would start out on his journey westward. A kitschy blonde screeched from the soda fountain to the soda jerk, bent under the burden of his glass head. About the values voters' pristine ahem. "Order up!" this person shouted and paused, appalled. I'm the jerk.

V. In *seasoning*

An apiary where the apes hang out, nodding their heads to the upright
bass's buzz. This person sucks a sugared lemon and puckers up for Mrs. Salt,
drumming her nails on a calcite keg. I prefer the ganglions, he thought he
heard her say. Some sort of animal, this person agreed, making conversation.
Ung! said Mrs. Salt unmistakably. It's a kind of nerve bundle this person
corrected himself, not removing his eyes from the stage where an elegant
ape emptied her shaker on a high hat. Ung! Ung! Mrs. Salt repeated, then
sucked, round-eyed, a cube. Anyway, this person said, taking her icy hand,
can you feel my heart pounding? He studied her face, its internal stratus and
radii, the rungs of the ladder leading up to her terminus and down to her
spunk box. An ape got stung by his saxophone reed and the audience clapped
and hoofed. I'm your animal, this person pleaded. His feet didn't touch the
brushed earth. But Mrs. Salt just went on grinding her molars, and her hairy
other hand spread like a stain on the paper tablecloth, a torn and sticky white
space upon which this person found himself beached.

THE NOVEL

No more poems, only novels. Novels are easy: you write one sentence and then a second sentence.

For example: The roadkill's black feathers fluttered a bit in the wind. Perhaps it wasn't dead yet.

The history of cultural overproduction is long and tangled but boils down to this: Mr. Edgar Leeming woke on the last morning of his life and got up and went out for coffee. He died later that same day.

Or: I began writing this on my birthday. I intend to stop writing it on the same day.

The girl you use for sex has a question. She holds her hand high in the air like a pale fringed flag.

If I'm a character in your novel what are the benefits? Will I be prettier, will it make you rich?

Her name's Sera. I take a long swallow of water while thinking about the question.

Shall I say nothing, an abstraction in the path of the projector's scintillant beam? The other persons are starting to fidget.

Just now in Chicago it's gray, spitting a little rain. The fans in the stands sing "America the Beautiful," "The Star-Spangled Banner," and "Take Me Out to the Ball Game"; it is ascending or descending, it's an order.

Everyone wanders around dazed and hopeful in the disaster's wake. Sera paints her fingernails black while I continue to say nothing to the room at large.

You were never real, I tell them at last. I needed you to be real to complete my own disappearance.

I can tell my choice of words puzzles some. I sit down.

Later in a lawn chair on the building's roof Sera straddles me in her strategic bikini top. She leans down so that her hair brushes my bare chest and whispers insinuations of death.

Will be, will be, will be. Sweet nothing of no name.

These sentences. They wrap themselves around me like Sera, like the serpent round the trunk of the Tree of Knowledge of Good and Evil (we must always use its full name), like the endlessly ramifying syntax of Milton who made English dance in Latin drag, making him the greatest novelist.

What we want most is to be heard, I tell the schoolroom, Sera's cardigan serious as her spectacles. We need to believe in a bottom to every well.

There's a bustle in my hedgerow and I'm alarmed now. Speak for yourself says Sera, walking out of the empty room.

Sentences imply a past, even those written in present tense. A long unspooling yellow tape leads me ineluctably back to the crime scene where I play every part but the victim's.

Prose makes it safer for words like "ineluctably." Sera is younger, will always be younger, be young.

Pose. Mistaken for Proust.

I've given her everything and how does she thank me? She won't even do me the courtesy of existing; she insists on the transitive; one must love something.

It doesn't matter how any sentence might be nude and fondled for anyone's pleasure. Backwards from the night window overlooking the city I retreat into the hot light of a hotel room bathroom where my reflection crouches to confront me, hollow-eyed, unshaven, a foreigner with shaking hands, protected only by his willingness to provide voice-over narration dirt cheap.

In preparation for the heist the dapper leader says, Our subjective is gold, all the gold in Fort Knox. Someone raises his hand—Don't you mean objective?—That's what I said, objective—But you said subjective—What's the difference?—I don't know—whatever you want—

Sera's not the leader but the crucial missing member like Shackleton's third man, like Harry Lime who's dead in the first half, risen in the third quarter, dead again at the end. Being then is polar and the novel's a doomed expedition to where the seas begin their rise.

The shortest possible novel isn't even a sentence. "For sale: baby shoes, never used."

Fewer words slip past a sentimental feeling. Invisible as a verb.

Character operates by indirection, as in the dictations of Henry James: It's a mistake not to claim a minimal unit of luminance. Lambert Strether, Third Eye.

David Foster Wallace wrote for Sera, then killed himself. In the interval he wrote famous poems.

I prefer his essays. I'd prefer Sera to look back over her shoulder as she walks away from me, but she doesn't.

Getting younger. That's no way to end a novel.

There's one way to end it. A man with two plastic bags filled with Marie Callender frozen dinners gets up and leaves this Starbucks, never to return.

Calendar pages ripping by in the black-and-white wind. Novels are adapted into films as a means of dematerializing time.

Films adapt poems as the camera lingers. But evolution has no goal.

Sera. Come back.

Prose crowds the margins. In which living has become, unthinkably.

WORDS WITHOUT ACTS

Of the mind.

Of the mind's Parliament.

Of the mind's Parliament sans Lords.

Of the mind's Parliament sans Lords in plenipotentiary session.

Of the mind's Parliament sans Lords in plenipotentiary session hereby resolved.

Of the mind's Parliament sans Lords in plenipotentiary session hereby resolved
on an action.

Of the loins.

Of the loins' machine in residence.

Of the loins' machine in residence above the Holy Father.

Of the loins' machine in residence above the Holy Father in his sanctum.

Of the loins' machine in residence above the Holy Father in his sanctum of
personal injury.

Of the loins' machine in residence above the Holy Father in his sanctum of
personal injury distraught under a blade.

Of the loins' machine in residence above the Holy Father in his sanctum of
personal injury distraught under a blade in prevention.

Of a chrysalis.

Of a chrysalis in the crotch.

Of a chrysalis in the crotch of a solitary elm.

Of a chrysalis in the crotch of a solitary elm before a bent dancer.

Of a chrysalis in the crotch of a solitary elm before a bent dancer spreading her hair.

Of a chrysalis in the crotch of a solitary elm before a bent dancer spreading her hair at the edge of a green glade.

Of a chrysalis in the crotch of a solitary elm before a bent dancer spreading her hair at the edge of a green glade lit from within.

Of a chrysalis in the crotch of a solitary elm before a bent dancer spreading her hair at the edge of a green glade lit from within the fallen fiery heart.

Of the man.

Of the man dealt a hand.

Of the man dealt a hand in the belly.

Of the man dealt a hand in the belly of a blowing between teeth.

Of the man dealt a hand in the belly of a blowing between teeth of the burn-clad hills.

Of the man dealt a hand in the belly of a blowing between teeth of the burn-clad hills beneath the roseate cervical moon.

Of the man dealt a hand in the belly of a blowing between teeth of the burn-clad hills beneath the roseate cervical moon at the center of a view.

Of the man dealt a hand in the belly of a blowing between teeth of the burn-clad hills beneath the roseate cervical moon at the center of a view perspectless and free.

Of the man dealt a hand in the belly of a blowing between teeth of the burn-clad hills beneath the roseate cervical moon at the center of a view perspectless and free from the fear of a hereafter.

❧

        drift
a ~   tethered
        moored

from the world-historical

          sofa

              driven   Miltonic stickpin   through our life's
crust

     tip in Satan's heart   the shaft miraging   Singapore Berlin Mombasa

                  and the angels on top, a
sprinkling

spiritual affect impales me   bipedal standee   throne for blood be seated

       spongy mass buildup   nuts to you

                 lymphing Magellanic clouds

     so far

        to goodnight   fair lyricism

Carnival gets cancelled
and the steam builds

❧

Pretend to it, chief sufferer. Magistrate marked by systematicity. Your specific gravity's been squelched.

All this energy comes to rest in a body hurtled back and forth between walls.

Osmosis passes through bone, bathed in the fire of labor. Blaze of bright hair round the conditions of its production. As means of subsistence for individual consumption.

What's to eat. Part and parcel of a compleat organism. Hoist meat! As it were, made alive.

⮑

To prefer the bruised fruit. Apple of sex, not a peach.

Parting lips in a landscape. To coordinate by the kiss, all roads leading to it. Dirt dampened on its way clearly to mud.

Nothing replaces heighth of a parapeted principle. Conditions of cellular production without a view.

"Stardust." Animal filament forms between our bodies. Perfecting the work or the life frets a string.

Gauze is a poor concealer. Spinnerets blind my eye to markets. The point is to apprehend the world: achoo! You're under arrest.

On your toes the red-rimmed inclines toward purple. Your face masking a future, eyes fixed on the back of your favorite head. Light uninterrupted by curvature bears the apple away.

A solar principle surrounded by the night it blinds. The new twenties threaded through with colorful overproduction. Who can stop the Chinese orbiter?

Who would stop. Catch rain in a rusty oil barrel, see depreciated dollars at work. Oxidation happens.

"Crazy." In your torn dress you follow the trail of ruby slippers. Bowery boudoir under pale glass slivers. A couch in the middle of the street.

Put that in your pipe and smoke it. The information is arranged in blue and green plastic bins, later to be hauled away. Stockroom fucking, mean what you say. Mean what you say, there's enough for everyone.

Fruited skin of harvest time wrapped in hot foil—that's desire. Archaic agricultural methods accumulate beards of virtue. Plain as your nose.

Slender's the least of her.

Hunger's attractive package if your dream were mine. The best song in the world! The last of Ithaca's only lonely, moated by what we know. A blow.

✎

Of the calisthenic withering of fat fearful flanks.

Of the pose assumed by Hindenburg at the instance of a spark.

General Blimp.

I pursue my own interests with ruthless and calculated disregard for the interests of others.

This confession likewise.

But a contract?

Blesséd bolt. Hook and eye. The boys come to carry it, all, away.

Little Land Lyrics

Ontology is the luxury of the landed.

—Lisa Robertson

1

Spoke and hotly the grass
so I go rocking on my thaw-leg.
What you've forgotten was never real:
the pain of return or a phantom limb's grip.
Recognition scene. Brand nostalgia.
A firstborn's counterlife.
Fallow, the glance
devoutly and purposing, everyday life
on a glass-bottomed boat.   Smote
and of a port in air.

2

Atavistic
            what lesson follows
to beat the band with a bag of sand
cartwheels of the itcher between soul and skin:
a dead logic persuades, dead letters receive
            what dead lovers retrieve
Asthmatic paper-horse, rocking horse, Mannahatta.
Plagiarizing myself. History of a short story.
Look up, look out
for the deliveryman's bicycle.

3

Spooky, there you are : a black cat's fur,
            matted and spattered.
Rain under the house.   Empty magazines.
A painted face maintenance. Hollyhocked.
Steam bellies up the bar, bachelor barrel,
ninety-nine cents a jar.
Out this window I can see the crack
in yesterday's ass. Hiss, wet Decembrists.
I call this stack of cans my follies
and this dark of evening my dark.

4

Abstract and title. Epiphenomenal rack.
Stalking a clotheshorse, dry-eyed theater.
What's busted is my brand : ceiling unlimited
                              and visibility zero.
And the time it takes to tell
smells you later. The jackdaw jaspers jadedly.
Early flowers propose a backhoe. Just
evacuate already and stop pestering me
about it. Scheme your genes.
The land was ours before the land's.

5

Dreamed a paper plane. Reduce, reuse, recycle.
"We're glad you're here!" Pleasurable association.
Through dim-lit alleys and breezeways
an agora sweater clings tightly to its idea.
Dirty sweet tooth on me, bulldog.
Unit of scansion,   soap bubbles.
A gay man plays a womanizer on TV, I mean
an alien plays with an atomizer. Good fences.
Play mumblety-peg with this microphone
as you wade my suburb's shore.

6

"Fables of Faubus" at Starbucks.
Teaching to transgress: the Justice League.
The Legion of Doom. The problem of the twenty-first century
shall be the problem of the line.
Recovered sentences, contagious shooting.
A bridegroom goes down.
I'm king of the hill I didn't build, like Howard
the Duck but bill-less.
I'm just drawn that way, Muhammed.
Boxing's been good to me, Howard.

7

To numb or name the node, the mode of this
emission, usufruct, letters of transit
signed by enemy generals, cold cream cheese churned
in the lap of the army's beachfront property.
I have drawn some conclusions about you:
lover or other, bemused friend of the family,
web browser, Mother Superior, a supplicant
jumping my gun. It's from before catalytic converters
so it'll run good on regular gas. Sly eunuch's smile,
ego scriptor cantares.

8

Alienation's authentic
on this episode of *Antiques Roadshow*.
At mouth-point death of the said, impaled saying—
splinter cell, pockets
of playa haters, beachless, limitless,
born to roll the bones.   Rap
snaps its banners in the upwind, Gregorian
chant goes platinum, boast it up or vanish.
Start up the one-man band, pooh-bah:
I'm lovin' it in this coliseum.

9

And never mishap
between us twain—   old Gonzago
blinking his ears.   Dumbo.
A curdle, a cuddle of political worms.
My ownmost possibility is the end of my
line. A tenor upstaged, floodlit. Airless
arias without music or voice. Particles of
the language, to do without. Family vectors
under my thumb, a vow hammocked. A thin
fire creeps my limbs in the eyes of a stranger.

10

Let whatever there is to come down,
come down. What you've built in me's
the pyramid's apex, all up around the economic
base. Failure words. Failure's a muscle
that wants work. Sobbing the abandoned laptops.
I have prepared for myself a meal,
lacking judgment.   Needs salt.
Perpetuum mobile, nature has a history.
Missed philanthropy, habitats die.
A beggar cousins me and I look away.

11

Perfection's superstructure, a narrative of
aw, oyster, shucks. It's ground, fine.
The boots are breaking the boys so come out and
give 'em all you've got. Try
drinking from a fire hose.
A class traitor clears his throat
for occasions. A space I make
for you to surround. You'll never take me alive
coppers. Penny-wise but pound-foolish, Ezra's
                        morphology refuses speciation.

12

When I was a woman my body thought,
passing notes in study hall. When my wife
thinks there's a pain alternating between ovaries.
O list, my biology, my Panjandrum.
Mortal, me.   But the mind
carries a plumb weight, soft as a water balloon.
Balancer knee. Paying out line. As Athena
gestates in Zeus's sinus cavity, he thinks
he grows his shazam.
I was born, I died. In the interval: sexed time.

13

Strange intermittance to admit what's missing
in honor of the half-alive absolute knave.
A certain discomfort in breathing, a cloud
lonely behind my half-closed eyes.
One that's neither man nor woman for bless her soul
she's dead. Reading German, better red, facing
Apollinaire in the basket of night.
Born alone repetitiously, sweet sixteen years gone.
It's worth money to be white
as a sheeted ghost on my memory's lawn.

14

highly lily
do rhododendron   annex
what's needed   the garden
of disalienated   alleyways
disparaged by helicopter parenting
what's made for me too, for to see
a child eating   his belly
but elegance too is fashionable
roam you Roman   nose
among planted petals   and burnt bulbs

15

"I dislike sweating"   who can admire
and who likes it   gym rats,
wharf rats   swimming strongly
toward our convenience   waving
out of sight   out of mothballs   under
my elephant gun   and shooting hat
the oak, the bay, the palms over
immigrant barnacles clutch head
ancestrally they find me intact
if I've got mine what have miners got jack

16

what minors have to realize is
the contents of this empty bag
displace effectively a buck's worth of text
messages   paper or plastic   redeems
teen spirit   outmoded   paradisal
lemmings   being   lemmings
happy to see you   but look inside
to find this filthy thing   I've always wanted
the choice between drowning and being crushed
a little leakage   between atmospheres

17

suckles superbly the supernal pleasures
as above, so below   so
I stood in the suntime   noon
swaying to the techno beat of skinned leaves
skating around my ankles   so
I flipped the turtle on its back new
things arise baking and beating in the desert
"maybe you're fed up   maybe you want to be by yourself"
I take root in this paperless age
it seldom rains in the here and now

18

a sad and triumphant rock band   elegiac gods
of the too-tight pants   lemon pledge
lollapalooza finds emotional rescue
for a dollop of mixed-use mundanities
I found myself a black-and-white extra
in a remake of Prince's *Under the Cherry Moon*
handling a pearl-handled razor reminiscent
of a certain unproven Darwinian plunge
descent of man beneath oilslick surfaces
the Mississippi breaks   my Internet radio

19

to your tents, O Israel!   build facts on the ground
as extinct honeybees once did
planting the stingers of their grand openings
in vicious children's flesh   bottoms up and out
a CGI representation   of a political economy
between myself as plucky six-legged individual
and sworn allegiance to the hivemind
I confess to wanting more of less
from under victimization's band shell
I do what a man may do   and no more

20

these trees have virtuality in their beaks
I mean the feathers of men are molted
"my life is exactly the same   except in Second Life
I can fly"   cue the amusing credits
from which melancholy has been scrubbed
still I insist on fossil poetry   to field
increasingly accurate simulacra
of a woman's hair in the breeze
chrestomathic shoreline   publishes Modern Corpse
every hair spoken for   takes flight

21

he wore a mason's apron and a bowler hat
thick-soled rubber shoes   and nothing else
a trowel for particulars
in one stubbed hand   cigar in the other
the crack in consensual reality we can only see
from behind   by the short hairs   black
sibling rivalry takes hold   straddling casks
of Amontillado this narrative is terminal
or chronic rather da chronic fort is strong
da is yes da is here dada blows its smoke into me

45

Compostition Marble

Love, the art of individuation.

—Catherine Daly

KIOSK

A walk from the garden into shadows of some length
collapsing the scrapers of a definite article
cast from the statue at our backs
that makes a face for the harbor.
Three years double meaning of a perfect fall day,
branches seeking a trunk of flame.
This shall be my Eastern
driving alone down the Henry Hudson
drifting across lanes at speed
toward Lower Manhattan, development, corporation,
toward the illusion of depth that's a fold
in our lucid dream of public transparency
and power projected from a thousand flowers
planted in a thousand rusted rifles.
But the dowsing wands pull down
and the line of volunteers snakes to infinity
with their pints of useless blood
from the center of the new Times Square.

                                                 If history
has exhausted us
as the copperwashed torch borne by liberty
has come now to spasm
like the muscles in a hanging judge's gavel arm
what can we discover in articles of war or confederation
(in the a that sheds its mastery)
to imply their effortful accumulation? The avant-garde's another kind
                       of preposition
as conjunctions function hand to hand
to buy the world its red-and-white dream.
Meanwhile children build bombs
and the perfect human has fled his language
so what's left of my ears is an instrument
to measure the intensity of the blast.

                                  Let the godly sort themselves out
to escape the drone-choked sky, to find footing in water vapor
made visible by odd altitudes.

I've met myself in a mirror
                    suspended in animal image
floating beyond my gaze
                    diffused in the island's albedo
that rains tongues and spires
                    onto our unprotected heads.
Surely goodness and mercy
        ·
                    are following too far behind,
waiting for the all clear
                    sounded from severed lines.

At a time like this the margins might be your only helpmeet.

From Manhattan's hard left the sun's straight line meets the hazard of
                                                        the continent

to start the Northwest Passage:

            ragged right the boroughs, the former Idlewild, Hal
        Hartley movies shot in Texas but set in the only America:
                the Hamptons unhampered, West Egg, Montauk,
            saltwater's long longueurs. Eventually the old world,
            th'unconscious that dreamt self-writing. Ruins of freedom
            mass graves and train stations. The Seine, the Danube,
                the Po, NATO expansion toward Sarajevo: fire flakes
            from burning libraries suspend red stars over Srebrenica.
            The end of the West forecast in geography, fanaticism,
                hospitality withdrawn. Stars of suffering and we
                the excluded consolation. Wrapping round about
                    over the Caucasus, minefields, oil fields abloom,
                boom: nuclear blackmail, the afterlife in a flash
                    of human hair, self-surrounded by the map's
            biggest blank blue. Hard a port, in fog, San Francisco.
                Peace. Peace and no use in a command center.
                No use in a needle over zero. Peace and no use
                    finding ground for the inflammable. Peace
            finds no use never minds never saw a tumbling
                                                    body's fall.

The vertical   burns
                          but what I see on sneakered feet
                                                shrouds the city.
Makes its field. The blank beyond the end.

Seriously it's depressing now even the glamour's
gone to Beijing. To get rich is glorious, to get glorious
belongs neither to the West nor the West
with a ditzy difference. Control ceded to a black box
and not even a cat's alive in there, just coordinates without conversation—
                                      last words
don't count on this digitized terrain. This is not a response,
not a language, not an action.
A little world that sparks and dies as hands
                                  brush in the street.
Narrow escapes at an intersection.
We go about in cars, sun up, what is empire to us?
We sing songs from a made-up China, join as masses
                                  to the margins.

The Hudson flows backward toward a history
                          that maybe meant something.
Voyageurs and pelts. Algonquin people
                          turning to wit and byword.
And Canada that imports everything
                          but power behind its borders.
In Paris I'll say I'm from Toronto. In
                          Jerusalem I'm from Vancouver.
Alberta is wild rose country—oh
                          to be a rose still red!
Un-American activities—pleasures
                          indefinitely detained.

/

There are still galleries in Soho if you know where to look,
while parts of Brooklyn are remembered for their grass.
Ferries find the suburbs—I'm crossing by E-ZPass.

Forever sutured to a birthplace, Mt. Sinai been seen,
Sloan Kettering may yet see. Yet first I breathed this air:
savor of wine and diesel, wind picking up,
a vacuum abhorred by English, tang of unseen sea.
Sun-barred buildings in Midtown, snow never white for long.
The stars as mysterious to me as the moral law within
my mother's breast where the smoke leaks out.
For two years I was a babe in the Dutchman's stolen boat—
one of those Stuyvesant would bar.
I woke up in New Jersey, model train on my bedroom floor.
I was born to have a bedroom. Manifest destiny had begun.

Kiosk from the Turkish for pavilion so picture a spreading tent.
"To picture" itself is an opulence—mere narrative's proletarian
like the brain that learns to labor only once it's taught
the words for feeling. What's for sale is my language,
batteries not included. To write it: pornographia.
To speak it makes a siren. Here I was, not am.
Yet we *are*.

      Verbs the only vectors. To-do

                                      matches my copy of "*A*"

But the cry is given to us   to utter from the nerve

      sea trials
      while

the heat death of democracy goes unimpaired
the dead father stirs in the unshared pie's crust
the tailor re-Taylored sinks in his mind's dust

O balladeers, fall prone to be the man
        of liberty sweet as tea

Is she really going out with him?

It's textbook   who walks from power

snaps tethers
   rich dad's prophecy

darkness demanding the aperture

          speed of cry

                         made for me

The sonnet undone
in shatters
at the bottom of the Seine

                       but compulsion's
         alive and well
                   surrounding our island
                    with its brittle shell

Morphemes deform in the mouth of a master

                       aus Spatland

while individual letters strain toward the phoneme

     ka   te   li

        sp   rn   ud

          lk   gh

   rm   bh

                shh

      on kiosk walls

          /

still a square, still bodies in motion on a molecular plane

metropolitan cantata of the cat-drowned century
lingering here with endangered pedestrians
"do you like hip-hop my man?
            is that an iPod or a hearing aid

think in language not about it
it's boring it's an it
dissolving under the tongue
it's a red scarf over your eyes
light not lines gets through

                        what isn't the case shall save us
                        the world is not what worlds

                                        CD only five bucks"

we must disguise ourselves as numbers for the right words to find us
I come in and out of hearing
a hand to my ear my tide

                        cries out *kill my landlord*

ranking angels put their spotlight
on the Lindbergh baby
to take that face away

who remembers the Beastie Boys
and their view from the Boeing's tail

                        /

            in memoriam a capital
            that never entirely was
            the Bowery stalks and snakes
            peripheral to all souls' quiet

Trusting in its tongues

I am turned aside from brooding
by antiques by outstretched palms
Bollywood music injures the air
an overturned wicker chair
and the isolate hum of faces
contemptuous of cars at corners

        renting real estate by the hour
        from a Starbucks window I see
        proud obstacles to flow
        eyeglasses burnt by the sun

We are women and men and children
eyes glued to what's called the ground
        versus
women and men and children
sneakered feet dangling in midsky

        all that's common to all is volume
        filled space between the ears
        dialing up the vacuum
        phones empty of our selves

scroll of a cello, its web page

                wavelengths of the Law

reside not in a doctor nor the man that empty clothes made

they go blind in the flesh
in the heel that loves a neck

            /

        that was the West   a vast horizon
        mountain punctuation   an idea of fresh air

        Here sheer verticals

give notion of a center
beneath our subway feet
the idea of a cone

and death from above
the anemone fingers brusht
a terrible red spring
when blood discovers the skin

fire and rust and oxygen implied

why is there always more sky
what do our satellites want

it's the surface tension we walk on
commits our young to beneath

Call it spring, scribbler
                 with   beside   your risk

what you know, you know

                            hath slenderly

                                                sleep no more

When the garden surrounds you
the world at any gate
oiling its own hinges
fouled with ivy, Amaranthus—

                    so hides the sun
            walking up and down in me

shed radiance   tumescence   gone green

                    takes root

in the conical event, streaming sand

particles of ray in your teeth

      as the city lets off steam blue as blue
      September

                                        /

A recipe for the sublime:
let x = x
then take a hammer to the =
not ≠ is the result
but a white space, static leak, a roar
till a new seen dot takes form
unimaginable and so perfected

                              solved, X withers watching this
                              from a concrete shelter window
                              on the edge of Alphabet City

                              a boy once

solve for the x
of the chiasmatic human back
bared   our   blades

         rebuilded

                    inked

                                    unwinged

STYLUS

From purely procedural traffic: mornings
the bridges teem and sway with the weight
of a concrete humanity—suspension swings
its arpeggio, precise by virtue of what it excludes.
Who'd have thunk it? to strike strings with hammers,
to ring the cables of The GWB by force of wind alone.
Arm and leg, upward and across—the jigsaw clewed
from above and street level, where horns, shouts, cries
concatenate into a picture that thrums the ears
and chest out and around the habitat
that shelters all vibration—this severed isle
on the mend, bristling with its own defenselessness.
Give me your poor to compose daily, architect-
onics of urgency, and smooth the map with your hand.

/

Sun starring the retreat from Moscow,
grass brightens the citizenry's sight.
The line that smartens up the sides of a cadet's trousers.
How tender we become at the wrong end of an arrow,
at the tip of the spear. These buildings, this statuary,
climb for the throbbing of a cloudless day
defined as death from above. As above.

Got you in my site
                    beam in my eye
under Larry & Libeskind's flarf
                           dagger answerer
to doubled permission

                                                 let me be and let me live

ex nihilo a third term   beyond skyscrapery
        and footprint

after memory after life

                    the slurry wall holds back
                doing, making, being, breaking

        Baking
on this intense afternoon overlooking Grant's Tomb
I can see here from here, as home and the enemy
stand always before your eyes. A saber connects us
in a fencer's flicker. Metal speeds the gazes.
Here there's earth birthing all of this, set in motion
by merchant princes. Earth that's given to every boatload
since water bore us hither. My father's
people an island away just out of range of the newsreel.
My mother a girl of six lands in Queens in her father's arms—
he wore her garment to his grave. God
was buried at sea, the fallen book unkissed.
Only the natured goes forgotten, given breath to bloom.
The literary is literal, a day's peregrination
in this unknown homeland, never at rest
between bounds. A kid asks if you eat your boogers
to épater les hipsters. Let us consider essentialist nature
as a rich idea we irrigate. So what matters moves.

                    /

            On dry land you know it's dry, you think of the sea.

            At sea's edge your life turns landward.

            A sailor sees the brim of land a horizon for his pay.

            Substance stolen to be regained once crowned out of sight.

            I thought the fad for pirates would pass quickly.

            Home is the sea once it's a scene for depleted imagination.

            Lubber am I on a rock by its pan.

            Girl takes shape on gray beach, salmon splash of her skirt.

            Fishermen perch in the margin with metal buckets of bait.

Joggers track back and forth hunting azure, downcast eyes.
Gulls fern and cry to complete the mental map.
The auld sea without lines painting fractals in repose.
The old lonely pitched at dignity by salt sigh of the air.
Perfecting an attitude to take to the interstate.
Persevering with the odd genitive, "of the breastbone."
To belong to one's blood only, to light on external stimulus.
The difference is broken.
An engine purling out of sight.

                                         What uses blood or shifts it, a
                                              system of relation

oxygen to mourn eating and patterns of decay

                        darkening, depleted

        to stand in feet of clay

Adding Dianas to Daphnes diaphanously

                    unhappy that I am   heave my heart
                                                          into my mouth

                    sing will , will , will

since quality is not strained

    nor the youngblood ill at these numbers

                    something in me dangerous

Admit the fraught flaming armature, the interplay of planes,
fire that taught you language heating the dish
of your coherence. Human tumult of clouds,
bare footprint on my retina. Head bone torn away
from the savage arm's imagery: dry valley of above.

                    I, Caliban, foresaw it,
              wastepaper driving the avenues.
              The isle'd been peopled else.

                         /

The final forsakes the final, the mystic awl bores me—
still I give names to each action, fingers gripping a cliff's edge
to give ten dreams to ten butterflies
turning pages with wings like fingers.
Dangling strawberries' dandle.
Takes flight the night's dive in gravity's rainbow
my body pours out like water

                    and the reel winds back

         (a reel is a dance)   (reproduces hole)

                    in its own real wind

         (a real is a coin) (subject to exchange)

These are images of images   plain as grievance

                         /

Surrounding the hero as if in a film—

Another extravagant reproduction number on the floor of
       Grand Central Terminal
Everyone whirling with her shard of mirror the better to

reflect what's on offer
An exemplary subjectivity uncovering the conspiracy of a
      handheld backdrop
Place/instrument: other people can be both, the axe that cuts
      the axe handle
The spreading difference you imagined your head bailing in
      and going under
The nineteenth-century catalog of types ferrying here and there

Radiant numerals counting off our national debt, pounding erasers

Paradisal clouds taking shape over the city seen from a distance

Velcroed now to those who might remember without aid of spectacles

/

Is it too late to pitch it light?

        A treat not a treatise,
        a trick for political economy.

Miraculous infrastructure glimpsed
      in a tanker feeding heating oil to a co-op

And what these islanders produce
        is only heat and light
        a radiant expenditure

Talents planted upright in endless rows

        in the night haze of human law
        guiding each to a minimal home
        breathing what surrounds them
        more than air   more than air

A newly minted movement

of dew silently silvering
the grasses of Riverside Park.
Condensation's force.

The comely margin of New Jersey
overlooks my permanent record.
I am new as skin
handed a hammer to strike
out a regenerated sound

that in black ink my love should shine

An Argument in 2004,

skipping the foreground as we're meant to

(odd seeing)

a woman framed by a government window gesturing forward

(her waters)

To bear repeating, the swan at swim two drakes
in the reservoir

(crowbar true)
(to put scarecrows around it)

something at least to look forward—Democracy, Part II:
this time, it's personal

(teeming blank sky of Amsterdam)

slight tension of a smile seen in profile
what's left of the Lower East Side?

the hand has not tasted—

"in one glance New York had disappeared," Geo. Oppen.

Sunday and sun. Brooks of light, the avenues
flooded. A few students, Dominicans, lean Africans,
a white woman pulled by a German Shepherd. Perfecting breeze
to sweep lamination from our image of blue.
Fossilized apartment blocks' blank gaze.
Decisions unheard from the street sweep the boulevard
sheltering animal hopes of a center. But no home
so face your fortune. Attempt lengthens but or as
as things to be believed. A smoking refinery
squats on the skyline—out of earnest talks.
Characters bleed in the rain or shield a face
for sleep. Stones to walk on, stupefying sun
makes it new, the scene. Where are people
joined to a voice? The wounded island funnel
through which we hardly dare to speak.

                                    Yet it's most personal, earth.

And whim is part of the process,
                         the glance is part of the process.
                         Each instant teaches its exterior.
                         The cloacal world unleveraged, unheld
                         but for the soapslip between each word.
                         Washed mouth. On upper Broadway,
                         faced hollows. Cadavers by chance and choice
                         pass by, tightening. I am, as passenger, alone.

But at 91st and West End,
seven stories of a twelve-story building
wrapped in ivy facing the sun.
Multitudinous shadows surface there,
fronding windows, shades drawn—
a life encompassing
separation.

                         So so long the city
                         that mirths music out
                         of unaccustomed silence
                         and rigors of autumnal light

                              not "des va-nu-pieds"
(ceci n'est pas une—>
                        this is not a drill
                        this is not a stimulation

                              /

        The gates are open
                              let evening come
        My goods are stolen
                              pure is my jealousy
                Beauty lies
                              but only to the truth
        Of what I hold
                              trustingly no choice
        But open palms
                              supplicating or warning
        Read dust there
                              the Law claps its hands
            Clasps stands
                              articulate a position
    Expensive melancholy
                              prescribes its own tonic
        Surgery particulars
                              reject context for solipsism
        Copsed residency
                              realizes the transitive
            Potentiality
                              a world that applies
        Itself affecting
                              uncoerced cohesion
            Say different
                              to fly from a capital
        Of fleecy skies
                              a meadow foreclosure

yet here is no elegy
nor foretaste of redemption
brute fact not always brutal
phenomena striking chimes

        birth seems beauty enough
        though home is to be won
        from scratched earth and sky
        and bursting the words mein herr

wir sagen we're parking
testament is cognate
in reading through the truth
of text as sign and portent

        wind setting forth
        from glass bottles arranged
        steering our canoe
        toward the compass rose

O spleen
fail to find me
the numbers unregistered, deliquesced

        (speak sweetly under the rose)

"Mais je t'assure, ils ne sont pas tout à fait mauvais," B. Cendrars

Passed hour of *The Passion*
sheer spectacle de sang
to forgive invention's sin

        I want none of it, no wheel

        but Ginsberg's queer shoulder.
        We need now a shout—
        my generation's gone to glass.

/

Plucked stung piano (*softly*), dust struck from the strings. But
out of the stanza endlessly breaking
into minor blocks and avenues
the grid collapsing into named streets of lower Manhattan
in memory yet green the crowds arrested
before snapshots of foreclosure, hands to the wound—
a million white shirts in the exploded sky.
Yearning for this now as we shovel 'em under,

                                                    shovel 'em under
the sand.

Do not overhear me, listen:
                            dawn suffers at our hands,
                            twilight is no more.
High-def TV versus the night of speech.
My metaphor carries no flame no longer:
                            noon obliterates.
In plain sight the human means less.
Only a cacophony, eyes closed, on Fourteenth Street—
only my heartbeat to answer the voices, crying

Save the city.

                            /

yes, world of appearances

its difficulty we make every day

we lie the sun up, sun down

real warmth as we see it

glare of an evening refining the Chrysler Building
                                        out of object

67

thrown like a vase it does not shatter

my glow, yours
                              from the space between
          made real

not the rip in things
                    that sanctifies

                              (trembles the shipping, afloat)

not temples, mosques, churches

                              (shed the foretasting choir)

                              theaters rippling satin
marquees light up a walk

                                        toward the American positive
                                        taking pleasure in between

and questions for no minister

                              /

          immortalizing punishscape   /   *inside cold dark fire twilight*

                              /

MARBLE

The only art is the art of artmaking.

Say it snidely so they'll know you're serious.

A dull spatter on a windowpane precedes vision.

Rain-precluded leaves, surfaces stuck to.

Or marking time, newly nearly missed.

As breath balloons a canvas to signify the instruck.

"To hand someone a stick attached to some strands of animal hair.

Do you always look at it in code?

Sheets of water assume a color traversing memory.

Parallax view from top to bottom.

At twenty I discerned some forms and mental spiders.

At thirty red shifted toward a halfway house.

Halfway gone with sticky fingers, sun blocked.

Thrashing to acoustic instruments open tuned.

Is so totally retrograde."

Happens to fall on my birthday, mercury.

Redhead, blonde, brunette.

/

Homeward sound:

imperial	empirical	empyrean	empeering
Mekong	me Kong	me conned	Macondo
dressed in	dressed sin	Dresden	dreaden
bored or	board her	bore door	toreador
infinite he	infinity	enfin du thé	finicky
Oedipal	et tu, pal	eddy pall	enter Paul
joke faster	Joad hasta	Yo massah	Jocasta
buffer her	butter her	bitter herbs	Buffyverse
carried off	carrot top	care to not	caritas
bagged hag	bad dad	banned mad	Baghdad
sins here	sincere	since you're	synth more
all's fair	horsehair	warfare	whore's fare

The letter giveth, the letter taketh away.

Saddle up
          to ride, seize the
                    boss signifier

fight heads, straight-legged

and fly on screens, find fixed movement—
        momentaneous

                anytime era

    needful ease   eases   reeds

    into heat sinks. We are animals
                  briefly clothed
      before soil bred of sun-
              filled crevices

In between we hope for reverence

           for just-in-time manufacturing

                cat's cradle between pairs of eyes

crossing the street
      millions
            to bathe in anonymous gaze

Stitched inversion, the city is man's.
Speech climbs high as my window: snatches
of Spanish, bus brakes. A word from the gut,
unintelligible. A gesture takes shape in my ear
like a hunched teenager in a do-rag
waiting to become a crime. Grief slips off
the windowsill finding no water to prevent rage.
Vengeance in the very soil: the land was ours the land—
Lace curtains for a peaceable sun, vigor of blue
softened, a contrail imagining bedsheets.
That glass building that doesn't transmit:
they built it to block your light. Home imagines
the Hamptons, home is green where you are.
Cross this line of death, dot the i in curriculum.

I dreamed I climbed Joe Hill last night…

Now grammar hems that paradise

                                        lends it definition

                        as water needs a wave
                                from dryland
                                                to see it

See me going under

                        parti-colored hands
                                        to generally strike bottom

versus a ship that sinks the land
                                        bound for the overseas past

                "reality and perfection are the same"

                        be it proposed: stacked containers
                                portside
                        as industrial terroir

                'gainst the wine that bears us
                                home
                        into our bodies as decanters

since every thing lies or sits as in a La-Z-Boy

walks or trots between

                                        and what we see through windows
                                                is only matter moving

                to make risible our visible notion

                                        of an outside, of fresh air

The outside only insists   even the open is broken

          spontaneous growths, cysts:
          the overflowing of organism
          freedom puts paid to necessity

and hitting up hard the need for a skin, its   difference.

          Irrigating free marks the former painter
          slashed the canvas object

/

Milked mercurial notion clouding the future's future
in the mind of an immigrant's child setting up shop
in the postwar firmament. Queens and kings seek a
scepter—let us settle for lean-to English. Kafka's
Liberty bears a sword like the dual mourning lights
stroking toward symbolism. Spell this craft with a K, cancer.
Survivor's not a name for you who burns the Norton.

          scriptable peace loses wax
          Roman records and Rodin hands
          deixis run amuck
          torches and villagers

he him and they
while the journey from 2 to 4
eats the day
Spectacle in the morning,
now in the afternoon
cut throats turn classical   , cherise

          and rerise,

          O sun of the twentieth century

/

          be born.

A green world her green eye
lights the lamp of Lucifer
O fellowing reed
in the stop-motion storm

                                        our birth, finitudes, love,
                                to slow instruction's approach
                                            makes Heav'n
                                            our bourn

                                        retire, radiance

Commas where you will
continuity. A fair
ground over Earth.
Donne's flea.

                                        isness without essence
                                        puzzles out a politics

            is it enough to mutter no,
                the city is   apparently

Words, things, the made
hypothesis ground.
Now to meet its *sistence*,
a morning.

                paradise alone

                                            burns down. I am
                                                this air. I

                share

                                an epi
                                center

and our life
        from the

                from

                                New York and Ithaca, 2004–5
                                Chicago, 2012

Hope & Anchor

ABOULIA

To what end have I sharpened
myself? I rise early in the frost and
axe handles of my little upstate
town. The leaves are alive with the
death that's on them, in the cores of
stems, white breath that pants on the
blades of the lawn, apparent stillness
intended. Oil hits $\_\_$/barrel and
the White House grows new fences.
We crying *shame* are erased, cry
again to be placed in a handsome
frame. This is the weekend demo
for mothers and old hippies, he
told me, on Monday they'll start
cracking heads. Safe on the pillow,
resembling the snow we'll sink into.

Ardency of the adrenals blazing
on the copperbanged roof of
a caustic supermarket. Misread
determination. Clang and jangle
outside the parking lot, Potemkin
shopping cart tumbling downstairs.
A message from the gonads: go.
Track the flight of the bumblebee
past the projects and the shambles,
haste sweetbittering waste. Tropes
for honeyed ropes strewn blinking
over the trees. On the St. Charles
streetcar a woman is buried deep
like nothing else in New Orleans.
My maw mau-maus me in the
mausoleum made from the girlie
magazines of my youth. That
yielded to faster honeys, false horse

latitudes. A woman represented by a skirt belled by a grating, great. You're with us, my bone china, you're one of the gang now.

You want it to mean something so you don't look too closely. You check your velocity and let the paint take care of itself. All summer the garden with or without me while I underlined words in a lawn chair, trying to turn them into keys. Capital coruscations, careful love, care less. Marx and Spinoza hold each other by the beard and dance the beats of a double canzone on Guido Cavalcanti's perfumed head. Jews who use tobacco are a dying breed. Our principal export is falling-down-on-the-job, our principal import is Bono. Thanks for the austerity cardigan, I don't think I'll put it on just yet. A black cat stalks the yard and the white dog whitens the glass.

Avast ye, SpongeBob, but here's a pickle in primary hues: what's mind might be prehensile. Lute strings snap outside the oratory in synch with the supplicant's libido. Art of underwater. Sword snags on a rictus root and the filibusterers' final hurrah. We're falling backward on our brittle golden hinds. Find a history for the cremaster muscle to gesture slyly at my gender: "A dandelion perfectly gone to seed, a complete globe, a system in itself." Seaplane lands on the Mississippi by a tanker spilling essence and peas. The ferry founds a sea-lane between bruised nature and a *Gemeinschaft*. Alligator sausage at the cafe. A wilderness of me encircles my campfire nightly.

If the future's less real than today, what do we live toward? If a rhetorical gesture's sufficient for us, how to expand its circle? With apostrophe I create you, the listener, and make a possessive to boot. Still walking up and down in the earth making bets I'll lose with God. Like there's no intelligent design: "You're on," says a set of letters. Correctly arranged they spell if we bring our vowels to the dance floor. A risky enterprise claiming land, backdating a leg to stand on. We used to wander not happily but with a certain cocked-hat panache. We inserted ourselves into a narrative and made it depend on our treachery. That started belief from the rock of apostasy and cast certain words into the corrosions of content. All that is solid melts into the hair of he who has ears to hear. It cannot be doubted, Socrates. I am your servant who knows nothing, who makes nothing, who dares not leave the room not facing you. The idol bows.

The Prelude whips to a stop, spitting gravel. My Huffy goes over a bump. This town is porous to my gesture, it seems to swim above the ground. Urgent burden of a nutsack mediated by heated mirrors. In the Navy the floor is a deck, the wall is a bulkhead, the bathroom is a head. Even the pirate navy yo-ho-hos its four to the floor. Wait till I play the race card tap-dancing on cheap headstones. They say poverty isn't marriage, at least not in this old grandstand. My dog is balding gracefully. My father hands out horny thumbs. If my features lack definition it's easier to bear your face. Carry me under your tongue and gargle your go-cup's light.

To make of reading a spectacle takes sideburns and suede—a tree to sit under, an apple in freefall. On the plane read the scene, in the car "Think different," on the subway to eat the apple giving thanks to regulations. Syntax devolves around who eats whom, right hand never left hand. "Why do they kill me?" Five hundred IOUs on five hundred squares of toilet paper. My father from a line of salesmen calls fruit roll-ups "shoe leather." What am I trying to give you but a little better service? Constituting a constituency to make love to is a poet's poor power—sweep of a hand to place pawn and king. As I ebb'd with the

ocean of life you were a narrow
fellow in the grass. Don't please lift
your hand except to turn the page I
should be.

First and only a redhead, a crown
on island experience. Nimbus of
the beachballed moon. If you can
feel green fire you can feel yourself
pitching across the lawn into your
clean home plate. The inaudible
body's clock puts out matches one
by one, not minding that it hurts.
A dunce cap, felicity, a snifter in
absentia. Rubbing alcohol, cool, it's
a cruel summer. Your silence before
the beatdown makes us call out your
dead name. And if tricky diction
hears? My body's an admirable is.
Clothes simulate an opening and
an envelope's meant to be pushed.
Sweat the imitation, Sally, plumb
the simile's plum. Purple life before
the decayed map of a simmering
flooded plain. "How long, O Lord,
how long?" Since *The City of New
Orleans* was a train.

LECTURE ON MODERNISM

The novels of Henry James descend from whence they were elevated on a brushed-concrete staircase. They smile coquettishly at a large flash. They are how do you say, apropos to zero. Their declensions fall on deaf ears.

The SS *Europe* steamed into New York Harbor and rammed straight into 14th Street. It is lodged there still.

Crepe paper velocipedes all over these islands, black and pink for mourning.

Lunch held a luncheon for a puncheon floor where hogs cool their bellies near Yoknapatawpha. Look, I found a decorum where someone must have discarded it. A decorum is a Roman coin, much bitten.

Then prose rolled over and stopped snoring.

A lecture takes the form of its hearers' mixed memories. One recalls the fuzz standing up on her sweater sleeve as a lightning storm approached. The one in love with her (three rows behind) did not notice this but attributed his own rising hackles to her resemblance to his favorite poem: Alfred, Lord Tennyson's *Maud*. Moral: memory is rarely progressive.

Every part resembled every other part except for Henry Miller's hangnail.

Declare yourself a genius and watch the bucks come clattering in! It worked for Gertrude Stein. Her rose still hovers over your blue book, a revenant noun and verb.

Get a load of that impulse control. We know why Jas. Joyce goes blind in the last chapter, now don't we? On the other hand Stan, his brother—now there's a soft touch!

"But why would you want to put your ideas in order?" Mussolini asked Pound on the golf course. He put a nine iron's tip to his lips. Pound shook his head and squinted at the sun. "From this angle you're better off with a sand wedge."

After Faulkner made off with her tricorn, Marianne Moore copyrighted Miss.

First electroplating. Then beaten copper. Then fresh ground pepper. Then snow began, snow began, snow began. White ashes whirled around spires and the people did not dare to look up. Color bleeds out of the scene for forever and a day. Architecture stalls.

A banner is completed by wind.

MATRILINEAL

Make space spectacular: you sir are no Jack Kennedy and neither was John a Jack. Stars on the insides of my lids in spite of light pollution. A political red hum: "Nobody else was there. Not even Billy was there." I was going to take my ball and go home but just then it split open in my hand, jointed as a grapefruit and as bright on the tongue. Inside was a diorama of my blue white house: pipe-cleaner pines, painted styrofoam roof, a flashlight bulb for night, cotton glued to the chimney top. And a plastic Greedo doll on the lawn—the me—pointing up at the stars—the us. Kids, never believe it: Han Solo has to shoot first. For what's solitary is what's compelled. A moral law's coy 'round phenomena, wills silence. Later: puberty and self-estrangement and a grandfather's numeraled forearm. Washing his hair in California a few months before his death. About my grandson's business, the toy deliberately destroyed, words coined. So a rigid hand relaxes and sorry about the mess.

YELLOW

The root of luxury is light. All need. All see. Chafed from stiff, a little death
flees from my arms and legs every morning. See you later. Walk to work
downhill, enter a zone of horizontal aspiration. That is, breath's visible as that
building they're building. We need again an unreadable home. Cinched iris.
Margarine light.

*

So I aspire to suspire, to keep respiring, quiring, not to spite this respite.
Uncertain animality's sufficient, I wreath a halo's briar. What protects my
paycheck from feeding bomb-bay doors. Oh to be a drone burnt black and
yellow with another's sovereign conscience. Oh for suffering, anyone's, to be
of some limited use. Help me open this jar.

*

Reaction of heat with oil: migration toward golden brown. Careful, the
plate is hot, and please pass the sour cream. New links built from molecule
to molecule make a blonder bond with matter. Thanks for being a table—
thanks for attracting flies. Somewhere a diorama of this moment on sale
inside a souk. Blood smokes shallowly under skin, a shame. The little meal
unrequited.

*

Sordidly the adverbs stacked chairs against the door, yet none could modify
the action. Brute burst boot. Yet yellow ribbon can't be crossed like a pair of
wrists. Can't see you for the streamers. Well dad I guess we got through it all
right, wrote Corporal Gilad Shalit toward home. He squinted through goggles
engoldening the enemy as a hand from heaven fiddled with his safety.

*

Hell no we won't won't go. Blinders on the Clydesdales huffing their way
to Canada. A claymore's a Scottish sword, a clavier's Johann's unworldly
smorgasbord. Sound, alone. Take flight toward earth like an arrow shot out

of mind. I'm living for ta-da. Shyly she raised her hand: but isn't it wrong to kill? St. Sebastian shivering atop a watched stopped classroom clock.

*

Four more years is fears: this endless ethnic music! Where possible La Contessa prefers to avoid the vulgarities of life and death. But bad taste and a bouzouki aren't enough to debone an empire. What's left is a fleshless fillet feasting on its own blue succulence. Revulsion is the point of this shotgun mike tuned to an empty mirror. We suspect a murder while wearing a suspect's veils, and fail.

*

At day's end I climb uphill to just miss the setting sun. There's a fire and imported beer to remind me of within and without. What's burning at the stakes. Photos say we're sorry we can't kill you out of the frame—still we rub furiously out your name. A lamp shades this ivory page, anonymous meeting place in which we confess that we are still afraid. Since the game has yet to be played.

VERY LARGE ARRAY

The world was new. Its egg, its cherry—"Madam, I'm Adam"—laid. Under
your bootsoles. A kind of frost on things was appearances. Blank of noumena.
The things sparkled mechanically in the just-born light. A chemical wedding
was taking place. A chimera sharpened its claws on the roof of my childhood
home. I lay in bed beneath the skylight and looked at the blue lozenge.
I rolled it under my tongue like a tiny gold key. Ancestry took place on a
cellular level: shtetl, town, city, suburb. Blank of terror. The displaced persons
in divided space (Alfred Stieglitz, *The Steerage*). Ocean blue, mothertongue, cola
fizz, arms crossed or outraised. Circumcision: the ocean. A world.

LE CIEL DES VACANCES

I was delivered to an idealism: no seashore. Though "gulls." Though
"flotsam." What use this deal of dunes to the shaper of the dresser of deal?
Exactly an avenue spreads its fronds to define a space for the eye to wander.
The eye that fetches an image home. Two notes collided in a beam to be you,
coughing. A trapdoor sprang for me and the ship went down.

*

Try to be less falutin': it's a nice place to visit. Brooklyn loosely mazes me and
finds me a stoop to sit on. The New Year breathes its senseless tsunami news.
A man on the radio carefully distinguishes between the sounds of breaking
and bursting glass. Drinking. Now it's all political, now it's getting all over my
hands.

*

No pies to divide sang the bandaged clerk. Love passes with Artie Shaw like
the advertising blimp in *Blade Runner*: yes, freshen my dystopia. The rain of rain
falls samely to be rain. Crowds collect on the dewframe. This loneliness won't
stick. So I fought for a preserve for the wings that sheltered your face.

*

Lost in place. Even cigarettes are honest in the lips of an angry drag queen.
Death dressed as a woman as usual. In my dream hand in hand we ran down
into the beach's well, our bare feet skipping lightly over pursed upturned
shells. A shadow haunts these memories. Overtaken on the way out just as
usual. Squeegee report at the mouth of the Lincoln Tunnel—escape with New
York down the eye-patch hole.

*

Pleasure needs no introduction to a man in a filigreed waistcoat bearing a
watchless fob. Dandy of the intellect kiss me hard on my chapped lips. We are
running in place to stay here as the wave taps us on the shoulder. Our eyes
caught by compacts in each other's manicured hands. Once twice three times

a lady gave birth: ladymass. Once a gentleman swallowed his eyeteeth in surprise at a dropped stitch. Bang buh-bang the bullets bounce.

*

Old wolf of the plateaus. Doctors under the influence. The presence of life on Mars. Europe, milk, hospice. Redeployed for the public trust. High salaries for high health. A power that needs no reminder. Repetition isn't rust.

*

Minima mooring, whale crawl, subsonic chaser. The dance troupe pursued through twilit shoals. Academy gymnastics leave emo in the dust. On wave tops. Invented shallow bathtub shook so noise ensures. Shock born bebop. Ocean crumples to become a flung cracked chorus of underwater stars. I hope we. I sin she. Banshee news.

*

Shapely I tongued thee, I found you foundered shape. Swimmingly I oared thee, I rocked you over the tidal. Sweetly I anchored thee, I bound you to promising sandbars. Heavenly choir buoy-borne. The ladder of extended arms in arrangement, splashed by your azure cynicism. Ladder of the folded brow. The discovery of underwater earth. We are moved.

MY POLITICS

I will describe only my own reactions to the glowing numerals embedded in the pitchscape. What colors were there? There was depleted uranium; also, cadmium blue to mark the graves in my brain. From the heights a valley and a lake that does not reflect. The human reflects, but not the perfect human. The perfect human sits down to banquet in squalor. He does a tiny dance with his hands. I see none of this.

Now I will imagine putting words in an envelope and sending them toward a place of use. Is that performative? Now I am imagining a red phone. Now a human twists on the ground. He's dead now, the lens buries him.

A little song between the teeth like the tip of Jordan's tongue. Place the person where I will recognize him, back to me, the face an unimaginable forward. I can only describe my reaction to the repetition. Oh. Oh again. Is it sin or symptom to be late? It is a mandate to be proud of, to go on with. When I began writing I felt it should go on. So we do.

Behold the flash of lettering, yet you must not see my face. Take these tears and imitate them without looking. Take this swallowed tongue and taste with it. There aren't enough words for surveillance. Or strawberries in a diplomat's bowl. I can only explain the obvious, which doesn't need me. That I need. The difference between tobacco smoke and air power. Summary tread of boots on the ground, where the humans are.

The lamp twists in the air like a green thought shot. The sun shows it to you. I am seated at a table eating and eyes burn the back of my head. This is noir and I'm the star, steadfast as that that will not say thou, shies its bow.

FATHOMCANT

Compose yourself. Stick on a tattered song. Your little yell in the alley, your suntarred sheets, just rippling. You are no gravity well. You are no one's gunned grave. But she's your rotogravure. Your black-and-white blueprints. Gold passes its musk. A cat in the air finds gravity, claws up, rains down, atmospheric. Of spheres. Of lenses. She was your sawboned of. Sought in love.

You lay down tracks in the path of gravel that led to a metered crater. The model train rode a thigh into the creekfed quarry. Geologically timed clockwater.

Aqualunged murk, chest on its back, pried aria. Aporia in the pool of your attention. Following your bubbles away from the surface of unrippled leaves. Someone's calling someone with your name. You named this gesture—not looking up—*upsourcing*.

Incalling.

SON

And he was a son, wasn't he, firstborn, given to anchoring, to rooting a man, the father. And he had a mother did he not who was the water roots need unrooted in herself. Straw spun toward goal in the apple light—he is fruit and seed between branch and earth. The sky suffers the ground to imitate it.

*

All light like luck comes from elsewhere, shaped or sacrificed or spilled among shadows that need it, leaves, to breathe. By your leave I am your son. By my caul I accede to sonhood's crippling rays. Sit down and taste this meat, bare forked from the soil you sprang from. A test of sibilance, serpent to say mine.

*

Dream of earth in town: all brown, the streets teeming with UPS men. Everyone tracks a package into and out of doors. All strangers exchanging gifts they'll never open for others correctly wrapped and labeled. I exchange a small box for a big box, the big box for a bigger box. When the time is right I find an alley to set the box on its end in. I scan the bar code and step inside.

*

Hair long as a woman's, my mother, but curled. An electric field's fluid inward. She danced round a cup of coffee, eyes down. Smoke drifted from the wrists of her coat like ruffs. And what are you to me, she sang, and what are you to me. Salted away beneath the table to hear her toes tap the top. And what are you to me, my son, and what are you to me.

*

A sandwich stops this singing. All afternoon he watched atoms get stuck on the window like flies. Every day the sun paints his house with another layer of thinnest light. The world becomes more visible, less accessible. Coming and going not going, wenting. As heat comes and goes with the forced air gone. The urge to count syllables. To count pairs of headlights catching the headboard, head-on collision with lights from the ear.

*

To play a part in the pageant bespeaks a bespoke inheritance: her hair, his lips. Her bones, his heat. Her mask, his mask upside-down. Her refraining kiss, his tennis strokes. A dry moistening of wet parchment, papier-mâchéing the skull. Which if made was well made to contain and interact. Hope's a bone home balancing on top of a parade float and an arm to wave its way. Paddling to spare the creek's child.

*

Given: a present. A perspective glass. Toward the son or daughter to be disclosed later. Behind a shadow getting longer: shadow of the coast, shadow of a sea. A singularity fixing to be solved by the discovery of time like parts per million of gold in a cubic mile of sea. You will be me, will to be yours, a went won't will when disclosed by an advocate. My end.

*

Some bark for that tree. Some lunge for the falling apple. Some wait for inspiration. The pathos of this is passing.

*

His egg is a jail I sprang.

POST-SECULAR

Glamor of the incompleteness theorem. Paused in a line of force: two people talking past the monkey in the middle, hands arrested halfway to his ears. Banal necessary connections: ass to seat, eyes to page, cup to lips, vibe to air. The medium is tall. People work at their computers stacking virtual bricks. She's a house. We are all turning whiter in the hillside light except for a negligible percentage. Christ is coming in a white apron with breasts behind. Sexual stick in the anthill, ringing pockets. Midst of this. Should I fly to Germany or France? Should I sail a fellowship to its end? Amcha—our nation—anguish. The young man's sotto voce—it's a woman on the other end. He speaks so's not to startle her. He flourishes rank privacy. Two black brows striving to be one. What itches: the pronoun. This embarrasses the floor, that's recognized by a chair. I came down on the volleyball, I just kind of hit it. Broke the beat. I did fracture. Six weeks, hand in this weather, my crutches slick. Adjustable like the boys of summer rising and falling in that video. A Henley's collarless shirt primitively squibbed on Gene Hackman doing the bullet dance in front of a garage. Blood suggests itself and we are progressively obtuse from '70s Hollywood to the greatest hits of the '80s, '90s, and today. Out of this country I'll think in sentences. Grammar will bare its thighs on a narrow pension staircase. Wo ist? Es gibt. Il pleut. Suggests a man behind it all, even this.

A brief history of empowerment. Why isn't folk music about the folk any more? If we sing along are we folked? What people sing in their cars: fiddy sent gospel. Something scrolls by like the idea of musical neighborhood. Does my lack of affect signal a hidden drama? What's the subtext to my noodle? Rules for improvisation: a large bad picture smashed over Buster Keaton's head. He steps through the window to star in American Gothic. A character actor bleeds on it. Simulation of paint peeling off weathered wood and metal. What sacrifices we've made for our microaesthetics of consumption! Where's the heroic worker's angular piston's potency? Equality on these terms. People walk by with cords trailing behind their backs to the places they are known. There's a small audience for this. Am I sufficiently literary on the bus? I missed my moment, I go on missing it. Last of the big-time bloggers turns out the light when he leaves. Rotten eggs. While this hand is moving the other one can rest.

Iron cagematch and the tragedy of the work ethic: spinning our wheels in solitary for the salvation of a social whole. Broken axle, snow: its sibilance blisses out the kneelers. Stuck CD makes a partial flutter, a melody perpetually getting up off its chair. A beat you can dance to, infrathin. I don't have to read the news if I don't want to. I can be poor and get a tax break. It's never been easier to make up your mind. Italy? Windswept plain outside Pisa, find Pound's misnamed mountain. I certainly do like dogs. Mount Misnomer, hung juries, legal lynching. Is there a music to this I don't recognize? If I refuse the myth of mother's heartbeat stacking iambs by the curb? The long I's peculiar to English, no? I prefer an O to funnel my residual religious feeling. Message in a bottle. Are they prodigies of faith, little Mozarts of credulity? Pleasure isn't pleasing. Am I interesting enough to write like this? Little dog, roll over. The author is born free but is everywhere in chains. Only the secondhand divides the unmemorable afternoon. An inch of accumulation expected. Times you forget where you are. Those are real flowers on each glass table. I hear it's a Christian place—see the saw over the door painted with "Give us this day our daily bread." A saw like you cut trees with. Acts of vanishing. Acts of vanishing. Repetition makes of us a style.

HISTORY OF FLIGHT

Thirty-eight thousand feet and there's ice in my glass. Into the sun flies
the head of a halo. Brilliant crystals up here and a network of blood vessels
behind everybody's eyes, pressurized to sustain thoughts of level ground. A
tickling. The orbiter burst and why not we?

Six flags over Texas and a Jewish star.

Leonardo's plan: to drop ice on Florence in the summer months. "Payload."
The whirligig met the thingamabob and they made a baby with wings.
Blue and oxygenated web that it's seeking from the nose cone. Inverted bell
curve. Berlin through a bombsight, the impeccable network of death trains
untouched.

Air power projects a spread hand over maps. Original dream from the air
sexes landscapes and flattens their crowless history. Switzerland of peaks finds
its ice eyed from lederhosen. The highest voice yodeling.

Eftsoons smoked spectacles heliograph at Kitty Hawk—the predator predated.
Was there any so American as right? Was there anything so Amercab as
night? Those bicycle boys defend their patents jealously, fight their rivals'
every feather. Wild spokes aflame with petroleum-glazed cards. True enough
soaring.

Dry bundled history set alight by winged tumblers. A smooth beast is born
in a blue-eyed sky while the old squinting century smokes in a parking lot in
Nacogdoches. Old-timey bankers shade their eyes cool green while a fiddle
string snaps in the stratosphere. Fair you well my lockboxed citizenry. Pop
will eat itself.

Surly bonds of speech: "Throw weight." A hurled rock flies until the earth
curves to meet it. Just in time manufacturing, that's gravity. Heeling and
toeing through the metronomed pine forest, ginger men search for the sons
and daughters of apogee.

Earth in our eyes finds our tears' perihelion. Goonight multiethnic American star. Goonight the peace process and the falcon's heavy hood. Goonight moon, we're in our blackout period. Telemetric seer O Houston the Raven, radio the news of what we've done.

SUN IN

The sun was now resting his huge disk upon the edge of the level ocean, and gilded the accumulation of towering clouds through which he had traveled the livelong day, and which now assembled on all sides, like misfortunes and disasters around a sinking empire and falling monarch. Still, however, his dying splendour gave a sombre magnificence to the massive congregation of vapours....

—Sir Walter Scott, *The Antiquary*

The sun fell in the ocean and we set out to find it. There was me, Andy, and St. Joan. Andy cast off and our prow found open water. Only a sail-shaped blackness distinguished the sea from the sea of stars.

"From land to land is the most concise definition of a ship's earthly fate." But there's no land where we're going and sailing's a poor simulacrum of a walk.

In the middle of the ocean we failed to find the middle. Even horizons were on strike. At least fresh fish were plentiful. Joan caught them on her spoonbill, Andy cleaned them with his pigsticker. I draped them on coals and picked them off again and burned my mouth on their glow. A silvered ember's slow going, it's a splash.

The ship knifed through the water. The ship scissored an unseen seam. The ship bridged air in the form of bubbles. The ship was something to live on. The sword of the ship ploughed a furrow. The ship gulleted to stay unfed.

Andy blew on his oboe, St. Joan did a dance by the brazier and flung her cropped locks to and fro. I sang: "When a lovely flame dies / Smoke gets in your eyes."

Facts are not persons and the reverse is equally true. Yet I ask you to honor this fact of our absence.

On the eighteenth day the water churned, the wind stopped, we began to rise and fall like sleeping. Finny fanged fish showed us their bellies in great profusion, flickering once in the light of the lamps hung amidships. A green belly caught that light and flashed it to its neighbor who flashed it lower and lower. The bright bellies spun in sequence to form a vortex which we joined. In a white gown and breastplate Joan stood at the taffrail, all eyes on her, and smiled before she dove. The virginal ideal of French womanhood sank like a stone out of sight. Like the ideal stone that dreams of uniting gravity and light.

For another eighteen days we swung from beam to bream. Fresh water ran low as did the cans of dolphin-safe tuna. Andy gawped from the masthead. I lay on my back on the poopdeck from which the whirlpool described the stars.

If morning comes without a point to assign light from and Andy nowhere to be found.

Alone from this bottle I write you: save yourself from seeking the earth.

Was it a fiberglass banana or a wooden O? What was the final sound: a rending of the curtain? A crumpling of charts? Decide on math or myth.

A dolphin bore me away and I dared not glance back at the ship I'd fired, its timbers burning free like a hand and flaming pencil. Felt its heat blanch the leaf of my head, inducing a greenness to grow.

I write this from the only island gratefully unfound. My limbs pygmied to the ground.

Solitude has named itself: *See*.

Iphigenia / Beuys

*

: And lives Electra, too?

*

Present

        your

harms

*

        felt

dilapidated

        hat

felt

        cored

fat

        wrapped

halftone

        healed

to be born
to be made

        in Germany

*

overland

    wrapped

    lure for feeling
    in the animal
    room

*

room for the observer

      participant

Archimedean lever of

      New York

*

"I Like America and America Likes Me"

1974
in an ambulance
its dark backward

      a master from Germany
      disabled by hope

*

utopia triumphant
work-life balance

      the life and the work
      perfect
      a brand

*

a man with
an axe

       held hieratic

       fertile
       with abdication

trees and tunnels
form a
wake

       : finish him

*

felting
woolen fibers
massy

       a cup
       of water
       draining
       away

world unseamed
       crushed

       logic of
       bees

I do you homage
I, a drone

*

: Within the holy shelter of thine arm
  The outcast daughter of the mighty king.

                    : She is a woman, therefore may be woo'd;
                    She is a woman, therefore may be won

          & the queen
          mirrors sex
          for herself

*

asymmetrical

          age

left ear lower

          than the right
          by a centimeter

night of stars
            encorpsed
from the mythic
Stuka
and emerged

          an English patient

*

life as deposition

          testimony of the body
          its weight borne by others:

your mother
your lover
the earth and air

by Holbein
by Dürer
the dead Christ is dead

but you Beuys, like a Jew
have respect
for images

*

: There serve your lusts, shadow'd from heaven's eye

*

hats off to reveal
a head made of gold

starts a hare
honey dripper

the dead too race

into more than two
dimensions
of drawing

stag's leap
the war

*

sput-sput
brut-brut
brit-brit-POW

ruhm-rahm-rAHM

awrrrrrrrrrrurrrrrrhhhhhhhhhhhhhh

ehhhhhhhhhhhhrhhhhhhhehhhrhhhh
rrrrrrrrrrrroooooOOOWWWWWW
eeeuheeeuheeeuheeeuheeeuhaaaay
rrrrrrruuuuuurrrruuuuummmmmm

urr
rrr
row
ayuto ayuto ayuto
problemo
mamma mia

sput-sput-wrr-eeeeeeeee

bowlerohhhhhhhhhhhh

oy vey oy vey hilfe scheisse shit
achtung achtung hilfe hilfe shit

booooHm

pheeeeeeeeeeeeeewwwwwwm
boooooooOOOOOOOOOOO

                                        oom

sprit-sprit-kuff

blablabraBOOOOOOOOOM
brabrafuckingBOOOOOOM

scheisse

ji-ji ji-ji ji-ji ji-ji jig jug jig

flux flack fluxus em em Emmett

BOOM

ahhhhh
aahhhh
aaahhh
aaaahh
aaaaah
pheee   phew   boom
pra   pra   boom

Al Hansen Joseph Beuys Stuka Bomber Piece 1989

*

the cymbals crashed
the horse's hoof

this logic of the organic like a
strong oak tree
planted in Hitler's heart

*

he is carried away
for the demonstration

        the animals await him
        dead listeners
        in a landscape

stag, hare, swan, sheep, bee-
flung viscous substance
flowing
in the well between us

        standing to our knees
        in sweetness
        undecayed

        the smeared pump, pumping

Lohengrin
disappears

*

: Sorrow concealed, like an oven stopp'd,
   Doth burn the heart to cinders where it is.

so bandaging
the knife

*

so rescued by Goethe
streaming fate
Iphigenia
of the bloody mouth
Iphigenia
of the outstretched hands

*

skull of a thrush
cushioned in iron
coaxed from warmth

the dead, the dead

*

: He died his whole life long.

: The King sits in the wound.

low and green
depth perception

                    : Lavinia, thou shalt be employ'd

the animal hand
the animal encountering
the height of its hill

the spiral from Germany
up
or down

*

: Oh, sweet nuthin'

*

I am your camera
Joseph Beuys

The Barons

IT'S ITS

happening to
                    the grue of things
: no motet
Listening is an escape, but our eyes—
close them.
Like a king we must be driven to claim our blindness
come to grief to
                    see.

Rhododáktylos:
our own grasping fingers
pull down
                    the sky's lid.
The sentence takes its form
from judgment.
A body of Blake's, his back to us,
confronts the rising sun.
That is no sun. That's a death ray.
We are trapped, schemers, on this planet.
The robot companion spins his feelers,
                    compassionating.

Fly in its fly bottle. Invented
bonds. The army we have.

What happens under hand, under eye, under heel,
forgets being. Is virtual remainder
of arête. I went to the store—agenbite
of inwit. I came back
from the store.

These more than literary matters
                    trouble the heart.
From the start
I came from a childhood armed.
Am now very nearly a nude. Object

of an intelligence. Terrible light
takes what I love
to task.

Press the flesh. Sweat. A woman
in me lodged is my Ecclesiastes. For
there is, never, any, "they."

The child
comes down. The
                air—

The instruments take my measure.
Only bleeding

must listening to it give, what suffers

                                        it's

                                    caudex, its

                                                        tree.

SEEK THE FACELESS SUN OF BEING

To stand facing it or with my back to it, at the track's edge
Spot of warmth I carry always when the air is cold
The air is empty, it racks the clouds
Tourbillions overhead to organize the light
My back to it grand marshal of ungraspable systemacity
Fish suspended in lake ice all winter long
In my pocket a piece of felt I touch blackly
Without directing attention to ambush, death
Everything's indifference like curtains hung
To divide a large room from itself
Pushing through ghostly walls discovering bodies
Face down on sheetless mattresses or the crook of an arm
Flung to cover eyes that might not even be there
It was no dream I lay broad waking the busy sun shone in
In a bed of phrases I toss like a restless sleeper
Pressure of an a like an insect in my mouth
Tucked between tooth and lip grinds its isness there
Will the train never arrive? For never is its nature
I close my eyes to the open sun
The sun like the earth I stand on
Platform
To place a man's head inside a bell is a mode of execution
Cruelly usual
The scratchy tongue of a mother telling the kitten it's alive
The sentiment of nature unfolding in human breasts
Air is sun. Salt is sun
I make a pact with you, Walt Whitman
I burn in the nothingness of air

CLANDESTINE DEAD ANIMAL POEM

Real demons and demons figural.
My exquisite form takes the shape of my death drive.
As if you could choose it, your own scarlet A—
letter I absorb wholly, indigestibly, inside.
To write it throw the pen down also
and walk away. *Take a chisel to*—
Overdetermined killers in white suits
drift down the city's boulevards
whistling "Lillibullero." I spy
one from my high window, forgetting
to turn off the light behind me. He
looks up and sees a haloed
target. His face is a white worm,
his finger is a worm that points at me.
His bullets are the worms that warp
my heart, which wakes in stone.

In Spanish punctuation swings both
ways—root and branch the question
mark hooks into the soil of the sentence,
cranes its neck at the end and waits
for someone to notice it. Someone taller
than an exclamation point
gliding by like a waitress on roller skates.

In Spanish *supervivencia* means survival
as though chanting "I will survive"
made an anthem to life's
superfluities and excesses
as though what we survive is life itself,
its malign tendency to produce vibrations,
to be summed up as the movement
of its own clashing colors. To unsettle the mind
and peaceful body, set them both
at odds. Standing in front of glass doors
into which a cardinal has smashed

looking out at the patio the redwood
deck the fenced-in yard
beyond which California sleeps
and other states are altered
in the early early morning of that
residual mirror the glasses on my nose
somehow got reflected
the back of my own head
tensile and alert as others see me, feel me, see
me. That's what life
is like, a series of destabilizations,
unstuck time like fly strips
plucking us out of ether
while we're focused on the goal.

Looking back prospectively
from a city I haven't yet visited
somewhere in South America
in extreme old age with liver-spotted
hands lifted in benediction
or judgment—it scarcely matters
whether I or Borges writes this—
both blind and both rescued
by what survives the will to survive
the perdurable remnant instinct
at the rim of solar vision
at my feet in the twilight. The cardinal
has flown. The past
is a negligible burden
made heavy for a moment by
a snatch of song from a speaker
remembering Emerson
exhuming his first wife, why?
To prove to himself
a point? I *am nothing* I
see all. So too the tourist
is nothing though elegant
in his white suit and cravat

black spectacles concealing his eyes
a newspaper folded on the table
of an ordinary cafe.
At the margins of all that life
still wetting and drying his mouth
romancing his own language
which he can no longer read
nor speak. Yet a letter:
I know you and will have known you,
reader listener my daughter
I will say I know you from somewhere
in the tumble of foreign languages.
I know you and will not guess.
A sojourn names me properly
until these futures return to sleep.

"THOUGH HE WAS SOMETIMES INSANE AND I WAS NOT THAT"

(Leslie Scalapino)

I give you jet
of blood a de-hierarchized mystification
of unrestricted ugly gonads pluralistic
scorpions finding their way to the birth
canal of the tired old virgin/whore (call
your mother) for that which cannot be staged
in sheer white space and room tone
spattered by braniac intestine
warfare how young actors are
running and colliding on a thrust
stage at any given movement out of the game
and into the stalls where coats or laps
conceal neither erections nor bloody flux
but the all in all of the seated body
that by amputation transfers pudenda
("shameful parts") northward
so the heart is the cock or cunt
the arms are legs folded protectively or
spread provocatively
the mouth and nose are the heart and lungs
the eyes the only face
the hairline the eyes seeing only notionally
removed from questions of sin or light
soothing always that darkness of the shoulder
the hair still hair
the dead-alive sexed-up profligate antennae
point of transference between whether and weather
until heigh-ho the wind and the rain
pushes down the bookshelf onto poor old Leonard Bast "mind
was meant exactly as writing to see mind (his)"
the out-of-doors eats the implied interior or
green room
where bearded forked creatures crawl blindly past
humping each other where they meet in filthy unplanned puddles

trailing assorted children behind them like withered limbs
half-birthing half-birthed well it's hell to audition
to be heard day after day
and find no home but one's own declaration
I belong to these words when torture is proof of life
I confess nightly just outside authority's earshot
off-off-Broadway off-off Alexanderplatz
off-off-Brecht's Mother Courage mopping
up the sick that makes the black space white
it all works by contrast by high difference definition
which yet as continuum never quite reaches representation
Mishima disembowels himself yet something lacks the color
something lacking in me the wise child replies
pulled to its feet at last the audience by sheer virtuosity
restored to tingling bodies severed stumps of applauding palms
for I love you and everything is beautiful
and you love me and everything is beautiful
who hasn't believed it
what is it to be mad

MATERIAL WITNESS

groin   water   hides trash from
meeting minds   climate modeling
shock of the Pacific   cubic miles of
redistributing   gold   whaleshit
electrons   stands   to reason both   get
up   lasers like skin   lost in what
the light conceals   in   an unaccountably
visible ocean   scaled body delivers
here a lake lone   unbuilt and unerect
and level   landlocked   the E. coli
coast   lets the I   consuming vampirically
go off leash to hump   the future tract
and snuffle and get   digested and released
its fur wet   cold   bitter organ
put a price on it for price   tags boulders and sand
requires a field   like human graffiti
intelligibly   fallible   fishery
there are no Atlantic   waves of mutilated
salmon   pain   nouns verb
convicts us   the visible
victory with   maps of no one's mind
you   you want fries so   no one decided
that   pressure's on   to frame the empty
Lincoln   license plates   pretty
pennies   state   secrets ventilate a time
of siege surprises   children need
a seat   one   to grow   to sleep
hundred nights   fifty   flatbed dreams   one
ten   reason not the   need for
righteous   deathlessness   uncanny
man up at dawn   until the itch itself
wakes in the cell   to find intellectual light
on wavering green   fields questions   leans
stems   fallible   back to life
rushing in   the gap I knows   is known
from weather   is level water

THE BARONS

In the time of ever more rapid diffusion and dispersal of truly humanistic termini
The time of collective seizure of rapidly diminishing carbon cores
The time of the barons in their towers growing fatter unto death hooked up to
dizzying interconnected internet spirals of IVs sucking everybody's placenta dry
Aka your milkshake aka my humps
In the time of dominoes laid from one end of the asylum to the other
The time of male whores who can't catch a break
Time of the underground economies trading hot licks for rapid desertification
Time of distant thunder
Time of the perpetual El Niño
Time of rain filling the abandoned movie house and everything picturesque and
prepared for the ancestors
Ancestor life the only scale that matters now the scale of the illegible the
illiterate the unread
Not just a Hitler but many come-Hitlers in the twilight bathrooms of the barons,
making their dicks look small
Being now of sound mind and sound body I, thirty-nine years of age
brimming with half-spent undessicated nougat-rich mortality
Say unto thee children, Burn the motherfucker down

*

Now you've written something and given birth to a critique
First critique says it's in your mind time and space
Second critique says you know very well what to do
Third critique says there's no arguing the taste of this poem yet you'll go on
wanting to
Mid-5 a.m. midfuture sleeping families strap on the masks
Air conditioners gust on outside dark houses disturbing the rats
Electromagnetic impulses making the circuit of the only world
I thought gnawing my own leg off would be one way out of the trap
Then I thought dying in the attempt would be another, truer way.

*

Burn baby burn that's the only spirit that matters
Literally burn the baby endless fields of fucked burning babies

The barons walk the line innocuous and off the rack
They're with you tonight in this room they're with you tonight in your
        televised bed
They're with you tonight in Rockland they're with you on your tax forms
Just because it's freaking obvious doesn't make it untrue
Why this is hell nor am I out of it—master the line of Mephistopheles

*

My mind won't let me rest until I record here what I've seen
Four lines of fire razing the land at slightly different rates
Parallel lines with just enough space between to make a vista
There's no point in making your planet a hell unless you'll have a view
The first line is rapid and distills a smokeless flame visible from airplanes
Mapping the earth's abstract grid a seamless seam running the cornfields
Second line moves more slowly and mostly invisibly wastes the sky
The third line makes lots of stops punctiliously burning each city from the
        outside in
From suburbs of immigrants and favelas like nooses tightening around the
        necks of people that look like me
That one sets fires at random it takes a long view to see the line
The fourth line is last and moves more slowly than the senses can detect yet
        rapidly becoming irreversible
It's this one that scares me motherfuckers it's the hellhound on my trail
Close my eyes and I see it spiraling from the horizon flames a mile high
        crisping everything
Rendering the ground a fertile-seeming black casting down towers and malls
        into architecture
Blown back by the slo-mo blast that is eating bit by bit my halo and wings
Eyes shielded from burning pitch and grit solely by remaining open
Back-drafted into a future built on the continuous present of ruination
YOUR NAME HERE thou shouldst be alive at this hour

*

Burn, baby, burn. Commas serve the deficit of reason.
I'm an attention-deficit hawk I say we have our eyes and lips sewn shut
I'm a suburban father with invisible tattoos on my body
Which small or midsize SUVs have a column-mounted shifter?

Be inspired. Great selection. Our instinct is to catch the baby.
Drop the old ones into their holes. This life is a Viking funeral.
Like speeches made by law into public address systems that render the words
          unintelligible.
True of every platform. The railroad rides upon us.
The appearance of full stops serves the appearance of rhetoric.
An argument in 1934. Young men are so young.
The appearance of caesuras serve the appearance of violent birth
Subdued to softer adverbs. Mechanically. Psychometrically.
Pastoral a function of our language. Groves are generative grammar.
The trees of truth cut down. "Tree in the ear," Wunderbaum.
Inverted tree of an underwater oil surge.
Its roots come grasping for us.
And all tomorrows surfacing.

*

Let prose handle the inwardness that personal history sells
Let the poem spiral outward like the kraken in secret thunderdome with
          Leviathan
Pulling the unread and unseen into mutual unequal struggle
Game of the corporate state hides the identity of the barons
Preaching to monster trucks to pinecones to stacks of burning children's books
Listening respectfully to their own beards the powerful uneducated persons
The fire lines are racing which will be first to reach the goal
The end of every burning

*

"A man who wails is not a dancing bear"
And a dancing bear isn't a bear and it isn't dancing
It's an it for our fascinated contemplation layers of years like Band-Aids
Now and of an age that surpasses ours in cruelty
Since cruelty requires attention that endangered natural resource
The bear in its Elizabethan ruff its fur and privates torn by pit bulls
Baited on its hind legs beats its chest with claws for the spectators
Who stand in a ring, backs turned
I like to go to the game and listen to it on the radio
I like to be larger than life and vanish on your retina screen

*

Seeing is material and being seen is spiritual
The more you walk the streets invisibly the closer you are to death
Rich reality of death foaming in bones and capillaries
Death shining at a millimeter's distance from every moment of skin
I think I'll buy a malted for the writers in Ghana these days
No one is deader than the reader more material sunk in aliveness
The barons are angels shining their bodies themselves are halos
Eyes uplifted to live feeds tracking the movements of material witnesses
Listening to "John Wayne Gacy Jr." I am really just like him
If homicidal homosexual clown isn't an orientation oh my god
I am not a baron maybe a little bit baronet
It's my pleasure to serve the oligarchy by not mentioning it too often
Every time I click this link it's like I've gone to church
The contents of their stomachs are mostly plastic
Decay generates the only heat that warms an angel's bones

*

Let silence bring to presence. Silence. Silence.
There is still a little shade
Trees are noisy
Silence
Waiting to be killed
Bodies quantifiable
Whatever silence
Have it your way silence
I don't care silence
Depart from this place
See what you have created

&

see the barons
the barons unmade

SÆGLÓPUR

Gut of static hush the single voice venturesome and small
signal to noise the toe-tap adjustment
a Turner reality a Whistler's frost of decadence
filming whipped grays and blacks indicative of sea
fog rushing the viewer's 3D glasses slack
planked lines for a ship a dislodged mast
for the ear to cling to sirens mob the horizon
somersaulting breathless in radioactive waves
exultant the listener at the proper remove
rent by slow chords adjusted for inflation
triangular perspective which my vector identifies
with the black swan's soar atavistic capture
snapshot kingdom that friends me virtually
corrugated void so you feel every bump or
as they used to say ribbed
for her pleasure for your trapdoor undershorts
surprised by sin by fishy pomposity by spill
like a rainstorm overwhelming clogged gutters smearing
the window the power goes out alone in the shiphouse
after forty days the canned goods and dry cereal are gone
you try hooks from the windows baited with mucilage
roast what you catch in a fire built from carpet strips
gaunt hairy crazed passing the time by solitaire
the bodies in your basement have all floated away
so when the dove finally returns with the sun beached on Ararat
a whole neighborhood of suspicious shutters surrounds you

you know no one staggering to the post office

but there's plenty of mail

as for friends and family they can't even communicate

what it is to fall in love with your own private wormhole

to be lost in an abstract sea that might be world-historical

floundering or else mere drift of generational ressentiment

but it comes again plinking the solitary piano

spotlit on a stage introducing gradual compatriots

the human voice an instrument blunt or thrusting or edged

a knuckle of bells following the syllables of Hopelandic

out the auditorium tunnel to the huge double doors

that swing out over that sea

rising and falling with the crests of synthetic emotion

in touch with dry salvage tidal wave of time's future

endless lyric moment posing as epic bearing down

death to sandcastles and mandalas and ephemera posing as life

children rocketing away through the curtain of water

that comes down at last like the fist of my imagination

and when the thunder's passed and the AC kicks back on

the commuter train blurs by and it's time again for dinner

the vision of the ear again safely caged

three of its four feet shackled as they say in irons

and sorrow wrinkling the brow and savage jaws

of this lion my aging body hunched concealing its kill

I give you this little thing this devouring mouth of ribs

feasting on my own heart

nipples blind as pennies stunned by perpetual sun

beard of the shriveled groin unaccommodated by old age
climb the lookout's ladder to the peak of shipmates' roll
ritual dunking and drunking crossing the fabled Line
each man alive to living knowledge
of resistless forces and the matter we commend our souls to
as if the mind were a body hurtled through the windshield
into a desert intersection with bullet-riddled stop signs
I don't care I need it to be this emphatic
aria of the alone Werner's opera in the jungle
Caruso floating magnificent on a barge of severed heads
the ruins are spectral interlaced with open sky
the serpent like a satellite telephone slithers into her palm
sin calling sin to beam us up and out of here
pinging the party's moral location in geosynchronous orbit
subsiding like the forest itself into fields of farting cattle
like boots crushing gravel in the expanding situation
engulfing our increasingly limited faith in opposing troubles
a tired optimism keeps us limping trustfully along
while new eyes glimmer in the fronds all around
it's a necessarily incoherent space I call a landscape
consenting bridging one last time the amplified storm
from lifted voice to lowering
and a sense of potable water amongst the tumbled rocks
if a scorpion is necessary a bleached coral reef's waterfall
I fall gladly on sharp grass a paradise alone
the red face is rising pushing out from leafy territory
a brown face a pale face a face with no humanity

but a stunted sort of pity makes it possible to look

without seeing fresh capabilities in the crumbling of infrastructure

to carry us far down like a victim drowning his rescuer

fundamental to utterance are lips teeth and tongue

food for the ear with ears to hear

that's survival's reach and even it's not enough

I am free in the face of each fully manifested disaster

and that feeling's an addiction I mainline it nightly

we're all hooked on phonics spinning appetite for destruction

for as long as we insist on a beyond to the face

that regards us now cruelly or with a show of compassion

it's only a sea gone white as blindness

and the sea is not a desert

and the desert is no jungle

and what I must see when I behold the stars

is static of the city city

dictating to and for me

what grants us freedom

                    freedom's law.

Acknowledgments

Thanks to the editors of the following print and web venues in which some of these poems first appeared: *Aufgabe, Bayou, Denver Quarterly, Eleven Eleven, The Laurel Review, LIT, MiPoesias, /nor, OmniVerse, Poets.org, Wave Composition, Xantippe*.

Special thanks to David Baratier of Pavement Saw Press, which first published *Compostition Marble* in chapbook form.

Special thanks to Carmen Giménez-Smith of Noemi Press, which first published *Hope & Anchor* in chapbook form.

Special thanks to Kirsten Hotelling Zona, who published a suite of poems from this book, including the title poem, in the spring 2012 issue of *Spoon River Poetry Review*.

photo by Joanna Kramer

Joshua Corey is the author of three other books of poetry and a novel, *Beautiful Soul: An American Elegy*, (Spuyten Duyvil Publishing, 2014). He lives in Evanston, Illinois and is associate professor of English at Lake Forest College.

www.joshua-corey.com

The Barons
by Joshua Corey

Cover text set in Abadi MT Condensed Light
Interior text set in Joanna MT Std & Abadi MT Condensed Light

Cover Art:
Credit: © 2014 Artists Rights Society (ARS), New York / VG Bild-Kunst, Bonn

Beuys, Joseph (1921-1986) © ARS, New York. *Iphigenia / Titus Andronicus.* 1984.
Photographic negatives stamped with brown paint between glass plates in
iron frame, composition: 28 1/8 x 21 9/16" (71.4 x 54.8 cm).
Gift of Edition Schellmann, Munich and New York.
The Museum of Modern Art, New York, New York
Digital Image © The Museum of Modern Art/
Licensed by SCALA / Art Resource, New York

Cover & interior design by Cassandra Smith

Offset printed in the United States
by Edwards Brothers Malloy, Ann Arbor, Michigan
On 55# Enviro Natural 100% Recycled 100% PCW
Acid Free Archival Quality FSC Certified Paper
with Rainbow FSC Certified Colored End Papers

Omnidawn Publishing
Richmond, California
2014
Rusty Morrison & Ken Keegan, Senior Editors & Publishers
Gillian Hamel, Managing Poetry Editor & OmniVerse Managing Editor
Cassandra Smith, Poetry Editor & Book Designer
Peter Burghardt, Poetry Editor & Book Designer
Turner Canty, Poetry Editor
Liza Flum, Poetry Editor & Social Media
Sharon Osmond, Poetry Editor & Bookstore Outreach
Pepper Luboff, Poetry Editor & Feature Writer
Juliana Paslay, Fiction Editor & Bookstore Outreach Manager
Gail Aronson, Fiction Editor
RJ Ingram, Social Media
Melissa Burke, Poetry Editor & Feature Writer
Sharon Zetter, Grant Writer & Poetry Editor